Endpapers: Detail of *Boston in 1768*,
engraving by Paul Revere,
The American Antiquarian Society

The Art of
Colonial America

Shirley Glubok   Designed by Gerard Nook

The Macmillan Company
Collier-Macmillan Limited, London

Weathervane from Amesbury,
Massachusetts, about 1715,
Abby Aldrich Rockefeller
Folk Art Collection,
Williamsburg, Virginia

The Author gratefully acknowledges the assistance of:

MARY C. GLAZE, Associate Curator of American Wing,
The Metropolitan Museum of Art

LOUIS C. JONES, Director, New York State Historical Association

JAY E. CANTOR

MILTON W. BROWN, Professor of Art History, Brooklyn College,
City University of New York

ELLEN MALINO JAMES, Lecturer in American History,
New School of Social Research

EMMA N. PAPERT, Senior Librarian, The Metropolitan Museum of Art

DAVID SICULAR and CHARLES DAVIDSON

Other books by Shirley Glubok:

THE ART OF ANCIENT EGYPT

THE ART OF LANDS IN THE BIBLE

THE ART OF ANCIENT GREECE

THE ART OF THE NORTH AMERICAN INDIAN

THE ART OF THE ESKIMO

THE ART OF ANCIENT ROME

THE ART OF AFRICA

ART AND ARCHAEOLOGY

THE ART OF ANCIENT PERU

THE ART OF THE ETRUSCANS

THE ART OF ANCIENT MEXICO

KNIGHTS IN ARMOR

THE ART OF INDIA

THE ART OF JAPAN

THE FALL OF THE AZTECS

THE FALL OF THE INCAS

DISCOVERING TUT-ANKH-AMEN'S TOMB

DISCOVERING THE ROYAL TOMBS AT UR

DIGGING IN ASSYRIA

HOME AND CHILD LIFE IN COLONIAL DAYS

Cover illustration: Van Bergen overmantel, oil painting on wood (detail), artist unknown,
about 1735, New York State Historical Association, Cooperstown, New York. Photograph by Alfred Tamarin.

The Macmillan Company
866 Third Avenue, New York, New York 10022
Collier-Macmillan Canada, Ltd., Toronto, Ontario
Library of Congress catalog card number: 77–102964
FIRST PRINTING

About 1585,
The British Museum

More than one hundred and fifty years passed from the founding of Jamestown, Virginia, the first English colony in the New World, until 1776 when the thirteen colonies declared their independence from Great Britain. In the early years, the colonists were busy making necessary household goods. Later, as the wealth of the colonies increased, they had more time to devote to the arts.

About twenty years before Jamestown was founded, the English made several attempts to establish a colony at Roanoke Island in what is now North Carolina. The governor of one of the Roanoke colonies was John White, who was also an artist. Governor White drew realistic pictures of Indians and their villages, and of the animals and plants of the New World. They were published in a book that showed Europeans how the Indians of America looked and lived.

Richardus   Mather

Johannes Foster sculpsit.

The Puritans left England and sailed to America to be free to worship in their own way. Puritan preachers became leading members of the Massachusetts Bay Colony. A Puritan minister, Reverend Richard Mather, was the subject of the first print made in America, a woodcut by John Foster.

To make a woodcut an artist's drawing first is traced onto a wooden surface. The parts of the design that are to remain white are cut away. The raised area remaining is covered with printer's ink. Then the paper is pressed against the wood to print the design.

Another method of making prints was by copperplate engraving. These engravings are made by cutting a design into a flat piece of copper with a sharp tool. The depressions left when the metal is scooped away are filled with ink. The design is printed by pressing the plate onto paper.

The earliest painters in America wandered from place to place painting decorations on houses, barns, furniture, carriages and signs. These artists or "limners" sometimes painted portraits, likenesses of people, but did not sign them. The limners rarely had any formal art training and used English prints as models. They worked in flat forms without shading.

Henry Gibbs, holding a toy bird, is painted against a floor with a checkered pattern. Colonial boys and girls were usually dressed alike. Mrs. Elizabeth Freake wears a dress trimmed with ribbons and lace. Her baby looks like a stiff wooden doll, yet there is a feeling of tenderness between mother and daughter.

About 1670, Collection of Mrs. David Giltinan

About 1674,
Worcester Art Museum,
Gift of Mr. and
Mrs. Albert W. Rice

Ætatis Suæ 100
& 3 Month
Apl. Anno 1721

1721,
Massachusetts
Historical
Society

Anne Pollard celebrated her one hundredth birthday by having her portrait painted. She was eight years old when she arrived in Boston with the first Puritans. The portrait, by an unknown artist, is bold and realistic. The artist has given a sense of the lady's strong character by emphasizing her heavy eyelids and sagging cheeks.

Magdalena Douw came from a family of Dutch patroons, large landholders in the colony of New York. Wealthy Dutch settlers were particularly fond of having their portraits painted to decorate their homes and serve as family records. Magdalena's unknown painter was concerned with the over-all pattern of his picture. The girl's flowered dress, the table, the fruit, the arched window frames and the scenes outside the windows create a bold design. Backgrounds in Colonial portraits were often created out of the artist's imagination.

About 1729, The Henry Francis du Pont Winterthur Museum

A common form of house decoration in the colonies was a low, wide overmantel painting which was fitted over a fireplace. Sometimes the scene included the house for which the overmantel painting had been made. This one, by an unknown New Jersey artist, is a sporting scene showing hunters on horseback chasing a deer. The gentlemen in their wigs and three-cornered hats seem too big for their horses. The artist has painted all the running horses and hounds with their hind legs on the ground and forelegs in the air.

Late seventeenth–early eighteenth century, oil on canvas, Collection of Mr. and Mrs. Samuel Schwartz

About 1690, Worcester Art Museum

Thomas Smith, a New England sea captain, painted his own portrait. Outside the window a naval battle can be seen. Smith painted himself with long flowing hair and a lace collar. He also gave himself a large nose and a double chin.

Captain Smith's hand touches a skull, a reminder of death. The Puritans thought about death calmly, believing that death would bring them nearer to God.

The carved gravestones of New England are the finest examples of sculpture from colonial America. Symbols of life and death often appeared together. This tombstone carving shows a grim skeleton holding the sun and moon. Encircling the skeleton is a snake with its tail in its mouth, a symbol of eternity, or time without end. Heavenly angels adorn the top corners. In the lower corners are bats of the underworld.

Detail of Susanna Jayne stone, 1776, Marblehead, Massachusetts, photograph by Allan L. Ludwig

Harvard Hall.

Stoughton Hall.
2

To the Honourable
Spencer Phipps, Esq.
Lieutenant Governour of y.e Provinces
of the Massachusets Bay in New England
this View is most humbly Dedicated
By Your Honours
Most obedient & most humble Serv.t
W.m Price

The first college in the colonies, Harvard, in Massachusetts, was founded in 1636, shortly after the Puritans landed. This engraving of Harvard's first three buildings as they appeared about a hundred years later was made from a drawing by William Burgis, the first Colonial artist to draw city scenes.

Massachusetts Hall, at right, was originally a dormitory with bedrooms and studios for sixty-four students. Two early presidents of Harvard designed the hall, the oldest building at the college still in use.

In the center of the picture stands Stoughton Hall. Harvard Hall, at left, has a roof with two different slopes, the lower much steeper than the upper. This is called a gambrel roof. Six gables, double sloping roofs that form a triangle, can be seen on each of the long sides of the building. The belfry, or bell tower, is topped by a weathervane.

The artist has included a carriage with footmen as well as people on horseback and on foot.

1725–1726, The New York Public Library, Stokes Collection

About 1768,
The New-York
Historical Society

Churches and meeting houses were among the first buildings erected by the

colonists. Above is an engraving of the New Dutch Church, completed in 1731,

after the English had taken over the colony of New Amsterdam and changed

its name to New York. The church is of brick and has a rooster weathervane

on its steeple.

New York's growing wealth is reflected in this portrait of the four Rapalje

children of Brooklyn. The artist, John Durand, has pictured them standing

proudly, wearing fine clothes. Although the children are stiffly posed, their

youthful charm comes through.

James Badger, age 3, 1760, The Metropolitan
Museum of Art, Rogers Fund, 1929

Master Stephen Crossfield, about 1775, The Metropolitan
Museum of Art, Victor Wilbour Memorial Fund, 1965

Colonial children look like miniature adults in their portraits.

James Badger, holding a bird, was painted at the age of three by his

grandfather Joseph Badger, a Boston house painter. The young man with

the shuttlecock is by William Williams, who painted scenery for the stage.

Eleanor Darnall, about 1710,
Maryland Historical Society

John Van Cortlandt, about 1730,
The Brooklyn Museum

Eleanor Darnall of Maryland, painted by German-born Justus Engelhardt

Kühn, is placed in a formal setting with a great balustrade and grand gardens.

The boy with the deer, by an unknown artist, is John Van Cortlandt, a

member of one of the Dutch landowning families in New York.

Social activities of colonial people were rarely shown in art. In this painting by John Greenwood a group of New England ship captains is having a party at a South American port. The lively scene of sea captains dancing,

playing cards, eating, drinking, sleeping or smoking their long pipes was painted

on a piece of ticking, a material used for covering mattresses and pillows.

The person walking toward the door with a candle is the artist himself.

Detail of *Sea Captains Carousing in Surinam,* about 1758, City Art Museum of St. Louis

Begun in 1773, The New-York
Historical Society

Charles Willson Peale painted this group portrait of himself and his family. Peale stands near an artist's easel, holding a palette, a curved board for mixing paints. He watches one of his brothers sketching. Their mother sits at the opposite end of the table holding a grandchild on her lap. Many years after the picture was painted, Peale's dog, Argus, helped recover some stolen family silver, so Peale added him to the family group.

Peale lived in Philadelphia, where he organized America's first art school. He named some of his sons after famous European painters: Raphaelle, Rembrandt, Titian and Rubens.

Robert Feke painted this formal portrait of General Samuel Waldo in elegant dress.

It was common practice for artists to paint only the face from life and to copy the body from other works.

About 1748, The Bowdoin
College Museum of Art

23

The most talented artist of colonial America was John Singleton Copley, who began painting in Boston at the age of fourteen. Copley studied engravings of famous European masterpieces. He learned to represent light and shadow and to give the feeling of depth and space in his paintings. Copley was greatly in demand as a portrait painter. He was able to capture the character of his subject.

These Copley portraits show Paul Revere, left, and Nathaniel Hurd, above, dressed in their everyday clothes. Both men were well-known silversmiths. Revere, the famous patriot of the American Revolution, was also a copper worker, and even made false teeth and spectacle rims. The engraving at right, by Hurd, is a bookplate, a label which was pasted into a book to show ownership.

1760, The Metropolitan Museum of
Art, Gift of Charles K. Davis, 1946

1768, The Museum of Fine Arts, Boston

Silver objects were a mark of wealth. They could be melted down and made into coins when money was needed.

The Henry Francis du Pont
Winterthur Museum

John Hull and his partner Robert Sanderson minted the first silver money in the colonies. Hull designed the pine tree shilling which replaced Indian wampum and European coins. Above are an oak tree shilling (reverse side), a pine tree shilling, and a sixpence.

Benjamin Burt, a Massachusetts silversmith, made this tankard, a mug with a lid for drinking cider and ale.

Paul Revere created the famous Liberty Punch Bowl at left. It was ordered by fifteen men in the Sons of Liberty, an organization that protested against British rule.

The teapot was designed by Daniel Christian Fueter, a New York silversmith. Tea was a popular beverage in the colonies until the British put a tax on it, and the colonists began to drink coffee in protest.

The silver sugar or sweetmeat box at right, by Edward Winslow, was one of the most ornate objects created in the colonies. Sugar was a great luxury in colonial days. The box belonged to the Olivers, a Tory family who left America during the Revolution and took it with them to England.

About 1760, The Henry Francis du Pont Winterthur Museum

About 1702, The Henry Francis du Pont Winterthur Museum

The BLOODY MASSACRE perpetrated in King—J—Street BOSTON on March 5th 1770 by a party of the 29th REG.

BUTCHER'S HALL

Engrav'd Printed & Sold by PAUL REVERE BOSTON

Unhappy BOSTON! fee thy Sons deplore,
Thy hallow'd Walks befmear'd with guiltlefs Gore.
While faithlefs P—n and his favage Bands,
With murd'rous Rancour ftretch their bloody Hands;
Like fierce Barbarians grinning o'er their Prey,
Approve the Carnage and enjoy the Day.

If fcalding drops from Rage from Anguifh Wrung
If fpeechlefs Sorrows lab'ring for a Tongue,
Or if a weeping World can ought appeafe
The plaintive Ghofts of Victims fuch as thefe;
The Patriot's copious Tears for each are fhed,
A glorious Tribute which embalms the Dead.

But know FATE fummons to that awful Goal.
Where JUSTICE ftrips the Murd'rer of his Soul:
Should venal C—ts the fcandal of the Land.
Snatch the relentlefs Villain from her Hand.
Keen Execrations on this Plate infcrib'd
Shall reach a JUDGE who never can be brib'd.

The unhappy Sufferers were Meff. SAML GRAY SAML MAVERICK JAMS CALDWELL CRISPUS ATTUCKS & PATK CARR
Killed. Six wounded two of them CHRISTR MONK & JOHN CLARK Mortally

About 1739,
Colonial Williamsburg Collection

Because they were skilled metalworkers, silversmiths made copperplate engravings. The scene at left, engraved by Paul Revere after a painting by Henry Pelham, is the Boston Massacre. A group of Bostonians provoked British troops who had been stationed in the city against the wishes of the people. The British fired into the crowd, killing five persons. Among them was Crispus Attucks, a Black American patriot.

Another popular engraving was done after the watercolor painting above, by Bishop Roberts. The picture is a view of Charleston, South Carolina, the largest and wealthiest city in the southern colonies. Ships carrying rich cargoes moved through its busy harbor. Charleston's well-to-do citizens built splendid town houses along the harbor's edge. A great many French Huguenots, or Protestants, seeking religious freedom settled in Charleston, giving the city a French atmosphere.

1718–1720, Library Company of Philadelphia

This view of Philadelphia was painted by Peter Cooper. Philadelphia, a busy port and trading center on the Delaware River, became the seat of the Second Continental Congress, the delegates from the thirteen colonies who voted the Declaration of Independence.

William Penn, for whom the colony of Pennsylvania was named, founded Philadelphia. Penn, a Quaker, tried to treat the Indians fairly by paying them for their land. Benjamin West, also of Philadelphia, painted this picture, *Penn's Treaty with the Indians*. It is said that West learned to mix colors from the Indians. For a paintbrush, he used a goose quill which held hairs from a cat's tail.

1771, The Pennsylvania
Academy of Fine Arts

West was one of the first American painters to study art in Europe.

He settled in England and became the favorite painter of King George III.

But he never forgot America.

In England, West befriended other young Americans who came there

to study art. One of his pupils was Matthew Pratt of Philadelphia. Pratt's best-known picture, *The American School,* shows a scene in West's London studio. West leans over Pratt's shoulder, looking at a drawing. The names of the other pupils are not known.

Before going to England, Pratt did this portrait of young William Randolph of Virginia. It hangs in a house in Williamsburg, the first capital of the Virginia colony. Williamsburg has been restored to look as it did in colonial days.

About 1773,
Colonial
Williamsburg
Collection

1714, photograph by Wayne Andrews

One of the most splendid houses in the southern colonies was
Mulberry Plantation, set in the rich rice fields of South Carolina. Rising
from the four corners of the house are structures with flared roofs topped
by iron weathervanes. These suggest the defensive towers of French castles
in the Middle Ages. The design for Mulberry Plantation was probably
taken from a French book on architecture.

Simple frame houses were the most common form of architecture in the New England colonies. This one in Farmington, Connecticut, has a steeply pitched roof and a large central chimney. The house is of English traditional wooden construction. Its outside walls are covered with long boards called clapboards. The second story has an overhang which juts out a foot and a half over the first. The diamond-shaped window panes are set in lead.

Stanley Whitman House, about 1660

Late seventeenth century,
The Metropolitan Museum
of Art, Bequest of Mrs.
J. Insley Blair, 1952

The rooms in early New England houses were simple and practical. They had low ceilings to conserve heat. The sturdy hand-hewn beams which supported the structure were left exposed.

This room served as kitchen, dining room, study and bedroom. Life centered around the fireplace, the only source of heat and a source of light. On the table are plates of wood and pewter. Pewter is composed of tin and small amounts of various other metals. On top of the painted chest is a Bible box, a case for books and writing materials.

Members of the family sat on stools and benches. Chairs were reserved for the head of the house and important guests.

The armchair at left is called a Carver chair. It has a straight back formed by spindles and a seat of rush, the dried stems of grasslike plants.

From Seth Story House, Essex, Massachusetts,
about 1684, The Henry Francis du Pont
Winterthur Museum

Hardenburgh House, 1762, The Henry
Francis du Pont Winterthur Museum

This bedroom from a house in New York State has a low wooden ceiling with many exposed beams. The hangings on the four-poster bed kept out the cold.

A huge Dutch wardrobe with large ball feet is decorated with fruit and flowers. It was used for storing clothes, since there were few closets in colonial houses. The room also contains a flax spinning wheel and a cradle. On the floor is an embroidered needlework rug. The five pieces of porcelain on top of the cupboard are Dutch Delft ware.

Needlework pictures were a popular form of art for colonial girls. The picture at right is embroidered with tent stitches, short stitches slanting to the right, which entirely cover the material.

Heritage Foundation,
Deerfield, Massachusetts

1761, photograph by Wayne Andrews

$\mathcal{M}$ount Pleasant, a mansion in Philadelphia, was constructed for a sea

captain who made a fortune as a privateer. The windows over the central

doorway are called Palladian, after Andrea Palladio, an Italian architect who

wrote an illustrated book that was widely used in the colonies. The house

is Georgian, an American adaptation of a style named for England's reigning

King George.

Below is the front parlor from another Georgian mansion in Philadelphia. The elaborate doorframe and chimney front are richly carved. Above the fireplace is an overmantel painting. Highly skilled Philadelphia craftsmen carved the woodwork and the fine furniture. The furniture style is Chippendale, named after Thomas Chippendale, an Englishman who published a popular book of furniture designs. The pole screen by the fireplace was used as a shield against the heat.

Blackwell parlor, 1764, The Henry Francis du Pont Winterthur Museum

1765–1774,
The Henry Francis du
Pont Winterthur Museum

1769, Philadelphia
Museum of Art

The colonists made glass even though the English discouraged manufacturing in the colonies. The British expected the colonists to produce raw materials only and to buy their finished goods from the mother country. Nevertheless, Henry William Stiegel, a German settler, operated three glass factories in Pennsylvania.

The glass pocket flask at left was made by the pattern-molded process. A glass blower collected a mass of hot glass on the end of a blowpipe and pushed it into a small iron mold which had the pattern on the inside. When he blew through the pipe the glass bubble filled the mold and took on its daisy pattern. He removed the mold and blew again, until the flask reached its full size. This process had to be completed quickly, before the glass cooled and hardened.

German artisans in Pennsylvania made pottery called slipware. Many of the plates had a tulip design. The plate at left, below, was made of deep reddish-brown clay. The decoration was drawn with light-colored slip, or liquid clay. After the slip was applied the dish was fired, or baked, in a kiln, a very hot oven.

The bird decoration on the plate at right, above, was made by scratching the design in the slip. This type of ware is called sgraffito or scratchware.

At right, below, is a covered tumbler. The engraved design was cut into the glass after the piece had cooled. Much of the glass manufactured in America looks exactly like European glass.

Late eighteenth century,
The Metropolitan Museum
of Art, Gift of Mrs. Robert
W. de Forest, 1933

Eighteenth century,
The Metropolitan Museum of Art,
Gift of F. W. Hunter, 1913

oger Williams founded Rhode Island as a colony where all men could worship as they pleased. The first Baptist meeting house, right, and the first Jewish synagogue, left, in the colonies are in Rhode Island.

There were no professional architects in the colonies. A merchant who was an amateur architect built this Baptist church in Providence, basing his plans on a design in an English book of architecture. The spire of the wooden church is 185 feet high.

The elegant interior of the Touro Synagogue in Newport has twelve columns symbolizing the twelve tribes of Israel. The ark is shown open, displaying the scrolls of the Torah, the first five books of the Old Testament. The synagogue was designed by Peter Harrison, an English sea captain.

1774–1775,
photograph by Norman S. Watson

1759–1763, photograph Preservation
Society of Newport County

The colonists placed weathervanes on
public buildings, meeting houses, homes,
barns, mills and stables. They turned as
the direction of the wind changed.

This Indian weathervane,
four and a half feet high,
stood on the steeple of the residence of the
British Royal Governor of Massachusetts.
Shem Drowne, a Maine coppersmith and
woodcarver, cut it out of copper. He then
hammered the copper and gilded it, or coated
it with gold.

The Indian has stiff metal feathers and a
gleaming glass eye. He is shooting an
enormous bow and arrow.

Early weathervanes designed in the
form of roosters were called weathercocks.

About 1750,
Massachusetts Historical Society,
photograph by George M. Cushing

46

The German settlers in Pennsylvania were skilled ironworkers. They decorated iron plates for the sides of stoves with raised designs. Biblical stories were popular subjects. The stove plate at right shows Cain murdering his brother Abel.

The colonists used brass warming pans to heat beds in their chilly bedrooms. They could be filled with hot coals and passed between the cold sheets. Warming pan covers were often decorated with elaborate designs.

Philadelphia Museum of Art

1740–1760, The Henry Francis du Pont Winterthur Museum

47

The Pennsylvania Germans decorated birth and baptismal certificates with colorful paintings which reminded them of their old homes in Germany.

Colonists from other European countries also brought the art of their homelands. As the colonists prospered and adapted to their new lives in North America, they modified the traditional arts of Europe to suit their new needs. Gradually a distinctively American art developed.

1771, The Henry Francis du Pont Winterthur Museum